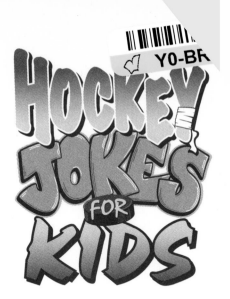

HOCKEY! JOKES FOR KIDS

Einstein Brothers

BLUE
BIKE
BOOKS

The Publisher: Blue Bike Books
Website: www.bluebikebooks.com

Library and Archives Canada Cataloguing in Publication

Einstein, James Allan, 1977-, author
      Hockey jokes for kids / James Allan Einstein.

ISBN 978-1-926700-47-2 (pbk.)

      1. Hockey—Juvenile humor. 2. Canadian wit and humor (English). I. Title.

PN6231.H54E35 2013   jC818'.602   C2013-906416-8

Project Director: "Mama" Nicholle Carrière Einstein
Project Editor: "Sista" Kathy van Denderen Einstein
Author: James Allan Einstein
Illustrations: Roger Garcia Einstein, Peter Tyler Einstein, Djordje Todorovic Einstein, © Photos.com
Cover Design: Gerry Dotto Einstein
Layout: "Sista" Alesha Braitenbach-Cartledge Einstein

Produced with the assistance of the Government of Alberta, Alberta Media Fund.

Alberta Government

cknowledge the financial support of the Government of Canada gh the Canada Book Fund (CBF) for our publishing activities.

Canadian   Patrimoine
Heritage   canadien

PC:

Contents

Introduction

Hockey is a funny sport.

No, really it is! Adults might not be able to see the lighter side of the game while they are busy yelling at the television screen for their favorite player to shoot the puck, but hockey games are filled with funny moments, crazy players and wacky disasters that happen every day on rinks around the world.

The best target for a hockey joke or riddle is your friend's favorite team. This is the easiest way to either make somebody laugh or get them really angry at you. Try it out. Find a friend who, let's say, loves the Montreal Canadiens and tell this joke, "What do you call five Montreal Canadiens players standing ear to ear?" Answer: "A wind tunnel." Watch how your friend reacts. Most likely your friend will burst out in giggles. Be careful though, and do not tell this joke to an adult Montreal Canadiens fan because older people ﹍nd to whine and complain and they might even ﹍ak down in tears when someone tells a joke about ﹍beloved team. Hockey fans in any city in North ﹍wa, especially in Vancouver (must be the dreary ﹍los like to whine about their team when they ﹍kn﹍k, just about every hockey fan anywhere ﹍laug﹍ whine about their team! So have a few ﹍re these jokes with your friends.

Chapter 1

The Greatest Game of A

The Greatest Game of All

It is a little-known fact that when Jesus played hockey, he was the goalie—because Jesus saves.

An Ovechkin, Please

A guy walks into a restaurant and sits down.

A waitress walks over to him and says, "What can I get you?"

The guy says, "An Ovechkin."

"An Ovechkin?" says the waitress. "What kind of drink is that?"

The guy says, "A White Russian, no ice, no cup."

> **Q:** What do a hockey player and a magician have in common?
>
> **A:** Both do hat tricks.

At the Pearly Gates

A Boston Bruins fan dies and is met at the Pearly Gates by an angel who offers to take him on a tour of heaven. As they walk around the grounds, the Bruins fan notices what looks like a hockey rink and asks if he can go inside. The angel says, "Yes, of course."

When he enters the rink, the Bruins fan sees one person all by himself skating up and down the ice. The skater is graceful and fast, and he makes moves that seem impossible for a mere mortal. And he has on a Bruins jersey with the number 4 on his back.

The Bruins fan turns to the angel with tears in his eyes and says, "Oh, my God, that's Bo Did he die?"

The angel replies, "No. That's God, but he's Bobby Orr."

Fun Ways to Make Hockey More Exciting

- The goalie removes an article of clothing for each goal he lets in.

- If the Zamboni goes less than 50 miles per hour, it blows up.

- Canadians must play in bare feet.

- Replace hockey sticks with live flamingos.

- Just barely visible under the ice is the frozen body of Walt Disney.

- At some point in every game, an exciting police chase takes place in the stands.

- Have Jason from the movie *Friday the 13th* skating around in his hockey mask trying to kill the players.

- Instead of an ice rink, use a huge red-hot griddle covered in bacon grease.

- Get rid of the puck and goals and make it a four-period free-for-all.

- During playoffs, players dress up as their favorite Ice Capades character.

- Defensemen must count to "five Mississippi" before defending an onrushing attacker.

: Which goalkeeper
can jump higher than
crossbar?

A

them—a crossbar
ump.

- A goalie with a goals-per-game average of less than 2.00 will have his water bottle replaced with Nyquil.

- Goals scored by goalies will count as 5 points, encouraging the goalies to leave the crease and join play.

- "Bonus pucks" may be added to game play at any time.

- One word: blindfolds.

Q: What kind of stories does Zdeno Chara tell?

A: Tall stories, of course.

At a Habs Funeral

At the funeral of a Montreal Canadiens player, the entire Boston Bruins team is paying homage and respect to the passing of a great Habs player.

As each Bruins player passes in front of the open casket to pay their last respects, a huge Montreal fan says out loud, "How come not a single Canadiens player has gone in front of the coffin?"

"Well," says the last Bruins player, "look where the casket is placed—it's in the corner."

The Great one

Wayne Gretzky, Mario Lemieux and Steve Y~~rran~~
all die and meet in heaven. God is sitting i~~s clair~~
waiting for them. God says to the three ~~ley~~
legends, "Gentlemen, before I let you in ~~aven, you~~
must tell me what you believe. Mario, ~~start with~~
you. In what do you believe?"

"I believe hockey is the greatest thing in the world, and the best sport in history."

God says to Mario, "Take the seat to my left."

God then turns to Steve and says, "Steve, in what do you believe?"

Steve replies, "I believe that to be the best, you have to give every ounce you've got!"

God says, "Take the seat to my right, Steve." God then turns to number 99 and says, "Wayne, tell me what do you believe?"

Wayne replies, "I believe you are sitting in my seat."

Q: How does Jaromir Jagr change a lightbulb?

A: He holds it in the air, and the world revolves around him.

Hey, Jimmy!

Billy and Johnny are walking down the street when the great hockey player Jim "Big Hands" O'Reilly walks past them.

"I recognize that man," Billy says to Johnny. "But what his name?"

"That's Big Hands," replies Johnny.

"Oh, really," says Billy.

"No, O'Reilly."

The Evolution of Hockey

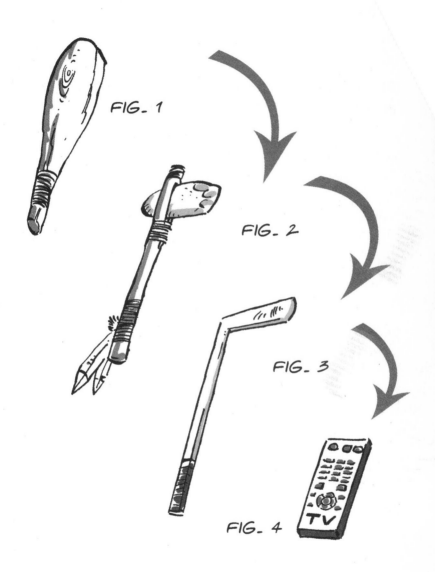

FIG. 1

FIG. 2

FIG. 3

FIG. 4

...her and Son

...nucks forward Daniel Sedin takes his son to see ...im play against the Ottawa Senators. During the game, Sedin asks his son, "So what do you think about the game so far?"

The little boy is quite excited but tells his dad that he has a question. "Why do some guys only fight, but you don't?" he asks his father.

Not wanting to look bad or afraid to his young son, Sedin explains that it is a measure of his skill and intelligence. "The guys who fight are actually quite dumb and can't do anything else. The guys who don't fight are smarter and more skilled," he tells his son.

After the game, Sedin asks his son if he enjoyed the game, and the boy says, "Yes." Then he says, "Dad, is Chris Neil a dumb guy?"

"Yep, he's a dumb guy," Sedin says angrily. (Neil scored in overtime.)

"Well, lucky that he was on the ice against you, 'cause he just kept getting smarter and smarter."

Careful What You Wish For!

One day long, long ago, early in the 1975–76 season, after years of glory with the Boston Bruins, Phil Esposito is called in to meet with legendary Boston Bruins coach Don Cherry in his office. Cherry reluctantly tells Esposito that he is being traded to another team.

"Okay," Esposito replies, "but if you say New York Rangers, I'm going to jump out that window!"

"Bobby," Cherry says, turning to an assistant, "open the window."

Pearly Gates

A man knocks on the Pearly Gates. His face is wrinkly, and his clothes are stained. He trembles and shakes with fear as St. Peter speaks: "What have you done to gain admission here?"

Q: Why did Jesus quit playing hockey?

A: Because he kept getting nailed to the boards.

"Sir, I've been a loyal Montreal Canadiens fan all my life," says the old man.

The Pearly Gates suddenly swing wide open.

"Come in and choose your harp, my dear angel," St. Peter says. "You've had your share of hell."

Ice Cream

Bobby Orr walks into an ice cream parlor. With some discomfort, he slides onto a stool and orders a banana split.

The waitress asks, "Crushed nuts?"

He replies, "No, bad knees."

Best Team

There is a huge fire at the All-Star game. Three hockey fans wearing the jerseys of their favorite teams are stranded on the roof: a Montreal Canadiens fan, a Boston Bruins fan and a Detroit Red Wings fan.

The fire department arrives and a group of firefighters yell to the Canadiens fan to jump so he can fall into the blanket and be saved. When the Canadiens fan jumps, the firefighters quickly move the blanket to the right, and the guy hits the sidewalk with a loud splat.

Then the firefighters call to the Bruins fan to jump. The fan tells them that he won't jump.

The firefighters explain that they hate the Montreal Canadiens.

The Bruins fan replies that he hates the Canadiens too, and he jumps.

Again, the firefighters move the blanket to the right, and the Bruins fan hits the ground with a splat.

Finally, it is the Red Wings fan's turn to jump. He says that he won't jump.

The firefighters say they really hate the Boston Bruins.

The Detroit Red Wings fan says, "I don't trust you! Put the blanket down, and then I'll jump!"

Listen to the Trainer

Joffrey Lupul gets off the ice on his first game back after taking a vicious hit. He motions to the trainer to get his attention and shouts that one of his ribs is cracked. The trainer tells Lupul that he shouldn't shout things like that. "You want to appear invincible and never let the other team know where you hurt, or they will target that spot," the trainer tells Lupul.

Q: In his later years, was the Great One in decline?

A: Yes, he was on the Wayne.

"But my rib is cracked!" says Lupul.

"You need to say something else," replies the trainer. "Say that you need another stick, or that your skate blades are dull, and when I get to you, you can tell me what you really need."

After returning to action several weeks later, Lupul is hit in the face with a stick, but he keeps his head high and skates over to the bench as if nothing has happened, even though blood is streaming down into his eyes. Lupul motions to the trainer and yells, "There is something wrong with my skates!"

The other guys on the team all smile, knowing that Lupul finally took the trainer's advice.

The trainer yells, "What's wrong with them?"

Lupul yells back, "I can't see out of them!"

With the Gretzkys

Wayne Gretzky is just about to leave his mansion to meet with team owners to renegotiate his contract when his daughter Paulina says, "Have a great day, Dad!"

Q: What do you get when you rearrange the letters in "Jaromir"?

A: Mario Jr.

"Thank you, sweetheart," replies Gretzky. "But why did you say that?"

"Because if you have a great day, so will I!"

A Hockey Hunter

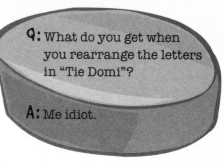

Q: What do you get when you rearrange the letters in "Tie Domi"?

A: Me idiot.

Evgeni Malkin goes hunting and has just tagged a deer as a game warden walks up to him.

"Where's your hunting license?" asks the warden.

"Don't know," says Malkin.

"Okay, you're under arrest for having no license. Help me drag the deer to the main road," says the warden.

"No way!" says Malkin. "*You* drag it."

Two hours later, after the warden has dragged the deer to the road, Malkin suddenly remembers which pocket holds his hunting license.

Eye Can Help!

After playing only a few games for the Canadian National Hockey Team, the new goalkeeper has already let in 25 goals. He is in a restaurant a few nights later when a man walks up to him and says, "I've been watching you play, and I think I might be able to help you."

"Oh, really? Are you a trainer?" says the excited Canadian goaltender.

"No," says the man, "I'm an eye doctor."

New York Fan

A man realizes that his new neighbor is a famous hockey player. "I've seen you on TV, on and off," he says to the hockey player one day.

"And how do you like me?" asks the player.

"Off," replies the neighbor.

Yes, He Is That Good

Sidney Crosby goes into the Penguins changing room and sees that all his teammates look glum. "What's up?" he asks them.

They reply, "We're having trouble getting motivated for this game—it's only Toronto."

Crosby says, "I reckon I can beat them by myself—you go to the bar and relax."

So Crosby goes out and plays Toronto all by himself.

After having a few drinks, the rest of the team wonders how the game is going, so they ask the bartender to turn the TV on. They see the score: Penguins 1, Toronto 0. After several more drinks, Crosby's teammates check the final score on the TV. It says, "Penguins 1, Toronto 1."

They can't believe that Crosby has got a draw against the Leafs all by himself, so they rush to the arena to congratulate him. Crosby is sitting with his head in his hands and wailing, "I've let you down!"

"Don't be silly," his teammates say. "You got a draw against the Leafs—and they only scored at the very end."

"No, no," Crosby cries, "I've let you down—I got sent off after 12 minutes."

Jock Fishing Trip

Two dumb hockey jocks are out fishing in a boat and pull in fish after fish. They are catching so many fish that their boat quickly fills up, and they have to return to shore early to unload.

After unloading all their fish, they go back out on the lake to fish some more. "This is fantastic!"

says the first man. "We should mark this spot so we can come here again."

"You're right," says the second man, who then dives over the side of the boat and paints a big "X" on the bottom of the boat. He gets back into the boat, and the men head back to the dock. Just before they get out of the boat, the second man says, "Hey! I just thought of something. What if we don't get the same boat tomorrow?"

Chapter 2

The World of Hockey

The World of Hockey

Hockey: the hitting, the slapping, the shooting, the pushing, the shoving—and that's just in the locker room!

The Best Fan of All!

Four hockey fans are climbing a mountain one day. Each is a fan of a different team, and each says he is the most loyal of all fans of their hockey teams. As they climb higher, they argue as to which one of them is the most loyal fan of all.

They continue to argue all the way up the mountain, and finally as they reach the top, the Canadiens fan hurls himself off the mountain, shouting, "This is for the great Montreal Canadiens!" and he falls to his doom.

Not wanting to be outdone, the New Jersey Devils fan throws himself off the mountain, too, shouting, "This is for the Devils!"

Seeing this, the Ottawa Senators fan walks over to the edge of the mountain and shouts, "This is for everyone!" and he pushes the Toronto Maple Leafs fan off the side of the mountain.

Hard Math

A hockey coach walks into the locker room before a big game, looks over to his star player and says, "I'm not supposed to let you play since you failed math, but we really need you in there. So, I have to ask you a math question, and if you get it right, you can play." The player agrees, so the coach looks into the player's eyes intently and asks, "Okay, now concentrate hard and tell me the answer to this: What is two plus two?"

The player thinks for a moment and then answers, "Four?"

"Did you say four?!" the coach exclaims, excited that his player has given the right answer.

Suddenly, all the other players on the team begin screaming, "Come on, Coach! Give him another chance!"

Proud Mothers

Four mothers are having coffee one day and bragging about their sons. The first woman says, "My son is a priest. When he walks into a room, everyone calls him 'Father.'"

The next woman tries to top her and says, "Really? My son married the princess of a small European country, and when he walks into the room, people call him 'Your Highness'!"

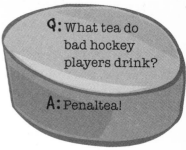

Q: What tea do bad hockey players drink?

A: Penaltea!

The third woman chirps, "Well, my son is a cardinal of the church. Whenever he walks into a room, people call him 'Your Eminence!'"

The fourth woman is just sitting there, not saying anything and sipping her coffee. The other three women look at her and wonder why she is being so quiet. The fourth mother finally smiles and says, "Oh. My son is a very large and handsome hockey player for the New York Rangers. Whenever he walks into a room, women say, 'Oh my God!'"

Iraqi Hockey

The Detroit Red Wings foreign scout flies to Baghdad to watch a young Iraqi play hockey in the new U.S.-sponsored league. The hockey scout is impressed by the hockey player and arranges for him to come over to the United States. Ken Holland signs him to a one-year contract, and the kid joins the team for the pre-season.

Two weeks later, the Wings are down 4-0 to the Blackhawks with only 10 minutes left in the game. Mike Babcock gives

Knock, knock!
Who's there?
Sak!
Sak who?
Koivu!

the young Iraqi the nod, and he goes in. The kid is a sensation! He scores 5 goals in 10 minutes and wins the game for the Wings.

The fans are delighted, the players and coaches are happy and the media love the new star. When the player comes off the ice, he phones his mom to tell her about his first day playing NHL hockey.

Q: What is hockey?

A: A game with 12 players, 2 linesmen and 20,000 referees.

"Hello, Mom, guess what?" he says. "I played for 10 minutes today! We were down four to nothing, but I scored 5 goals, and we won the game! The coach, the players, the fans, the media—they all love me."

"Wonderful," says his mom. "Let me tell you about my day. Your father got shot in the street and was robbed. Your sister and I were ambushed and beaten up by a group of thugs, and your little brother has joined a gang of looters! And all the while you were having such a great time."

The young Iraqi is very upset. "Oh. What can I say, Mom, but I'm so sorry."

"Sorry? You're sorry?!" says his mom. "It's your fault we moved to Detroit in the first place!"

Bad Manager

A manager is being interviewed after he resigns from a losing hockey team.

"Wasn't the crowd behind you?" asks the reporter.

"They were right behind me all right," says the manager, "but I managed to shake them off at the airport!"

Q: How did the blond fisherman die?

A: He was ice fishing and got run over by the Zamboni.

You Know You Watch Too Much Hockey When

- You think about what every sport would be like with a hockey stick.

- You can impersonate every NHL player.

- You can name the top 100 players but can't remember the names of your aunts and uncles.

- You keep track of every statistic of every player along with his ranking and points but you can't pass math in school.

- Your parents named you after an NHL player.

- During an exam, you map out the line-ups for the next game.

Definition of Hockey

Hockey is a game where a bunch of men skate around for two hours watched by people who could really use the exercise.

Q: Why did the goalie get fired from his ironing job at the dry cleaners?

A: Because he wouldn't get out of the crease.

Top Ten Biggest Lies in Hockey

10. We think the referee made the right call.

9. That foot-in-the-crease rule has really improved the game in many ways.

8. Anything said about Roberto Luongo.

7. Any news report that says salary negotiations were done in a friendly manner.

6. We think his agent advised him very wisely.

5. Don't sweat it, kid. We're just sending you down to the minors for a few weeks.

4. Our players never take painkiller injections.

3. I don't care if I am not scoring, so long as the team is winning.

2. Honest, Coach, I already did my homework!

1. This will only hurt for a little while.

In the Bathroom

The Toronto Maple Leafs and the Detroit Red Wings are in Toronto playing a close game. They are tied 1-1 late in the third period.

Just before a faceoff, Tie Domi lines up next to Chris Chelios and says, "Hey, Chelios, you're an American and playing hockey in Canada, right?"

Chelios puffs out his chest and says, "You bet I am, and I'm proud of it!"

Tie Domi smiles and says, "Then what are you in the bathroom?"

Chelios looks at Domi and appears to look confused. He asks, "What?"

Domi laughs and says, "In the bathroom, European."

Q: How many NHL executives does it take to change a lightbulb?

A: None, they'll only promise change.

Hockey Terms All Fans Should Know

Bodycheck: A way to test the rink boards and glass, for durability.

Enforcer: The guy who leads the NHL in penalty minutes.

Europeans: Skilled players who refuse to watch "Coach's Corner."

Gross misconduct: The bad behavior of very rich role models.

Instant replay: A way to prove the incompetence of on-ice officials.

Net: Twenty-five percent of the money that goes to the winner of a 50-50 draw.

Penalty box: A good place for TV close-ups of players mouthing swear words at each other.

PIMs: Rating system for unskilled players.

Play by play: The break between TV commercials.

Predators: (a) another Yankee team—from Peoria or Portland; (b) agents.

Puck: Nickname for the millionaire, now in jail, who sold Gretzky to another millionaire.

Redline: The mark on a new sweater—from leaning over a "Wet Paint" sign at the penalty bench.

Rink: The weekend hangout for parents with kids who play hockey.

Scoreboard: A place for annoying business signs and logos.

Shoot: What polite hockey kids say after missing a wide-open net.

Q: What's the best way to get a hockey player into a bank?

A: Offer free checking.

Slapshot: A movie poking fun at Canada's national pastime.

Stanley Cup: A trophy awarded to a championship team just before the opening of training camp.

Wraparound: The visor worn by Europeans, which makes Don Cherry angry.

Zamboni: An ice-cleaning machine that fills arenas with smelly fumes.

Heard at a News Conference

A reporter asks one of the NHL owners at a news conference, "Is your lack of movement on the hockey negotiations because of ignorance or apathy?"

The owner replies, "I don't know, and I don't care!"

Q: Why did they stop the hockey game in the leper colony?

A: Because there was a faceoff in the corner.

Class Exercise

A history teacher asks her students to make a list of the six greatest Canadians of all time. After 30 minutes, everyone in the class turns in their papers, except for Mike, who is still scratching his head and is in deep thought.

"What's wrong, Mike?" asks the teacher. "Are you having trouble coming up with six great Canadians?"

"I've got all but one," the student replies. "It's the goaltender I can't decide on."

Refs in the Wild

Two NHL referees are walking through the countryside, and they notice some tracks. The first ref says, "Deer tracks?"

"No," replies the second. "Bear tracks."

The conversation ends abruptly when a train hits them.

Funny Comments About Hockey

- A hockey fan is a guy who will yell at a forward for not spotting the opening in the net, then he'll head to the parking lot and can't find his own car.

- If a guy watches three hockey games in a row, he should be declared legally dead.

- Did you hear about the dumb guy who lost $50 betting on the hockey game? He lost $25 on the game and $25 on the replay.

- If hockey and exercise are so good for your health, why do the professionals retire by age 35?

Hockey Struggles

A rookie goaltender is struggling in the net, so the team captain skates up to him to have a talk. "I've figured out your problem," he tells the young goaltender. "You always lose control at the same point in every game."

"When is that?"

"Right after the national anthem."

Chapter 3

Crazy Hockey Kids

crazy Hockey Kids

Be kind to animals—hug a hockey player.

First Fight!

A kid comes home after playing a hockey game and proudly says to his mother, "I was in my first hockey fight."

"What?!" his mom says. "Let me see your mouth."

The boy opens his mouth.

"Oh, no!" says his mom. "You've lost your front teeth!"

The little boy replies, "No, I didn't. They're in my front pocket."

First Grade

A first grade teacher explains to her class that she is a New Jersey Devils fan. She asks her students to raise their hands if they are Devils fans, too. Not really knowing what a "Devils fan" is, but wanting to be liked by their teacher, the students raise their hands into the air—except one student. A girl named Mary is not going along with the rest of the class.

The teacher asks her why she has decided to be different.

"Because I'm not a Devils fan," says little Mary.

"Then what are you?" asks the teacher.

"I'm proud to be a Philadelphia Flyers fan," says the girl.

Q. How many Buffalo Sabres does it take to win a Stanley Cup?

A. Nobody knows, and we may never find out.

The teacher is a little curious now. She asks Mary why she is a Flyers fan.

"Well, my dad and mom are Flyers fans, and I'm a Flyers fan, too!"

The teacher is now upset. "That's no reason!" she says loudly. "If your mom was being silly, and your dad was being silly, what would you be then?"

Mary pauses for a moment to think and then says, "I'd be a Devils fan."

Q: What do college students and the Vancouver Canucks have in common?

A: They've both finished their year by April.

A Kid in Court

In front of a judge in court is a little boy. The court case is about the custody of the boy during his parents' divorce.

The judge asks the boy, "Do you want to live with your mother?"

They boy replies, "No, I don't want to live with her because she beats me!"

The surprised judge then asks, "Do you want to live with your father?"

The boy says, "No, he beats me too!"

Finally the judge asks, "Where do you want to live?"

The child says, "I want to live with the Buffalo Sabres!"

"Why do you want to live with the Buffalo Sabres?" asks the judge.

The boy shouts, "Because the Buffalo Sabres don't beat anybody!"

Is It True?

Little David is in grade five, and his teacher asks all the kids what their fathers do for a living. Some of the answers are doctor, firefighter, police officer, accountant and so on. David is very quiet, which is unusual for him, so the teacher calls on him to answer.

David says, "My father is an exotic dancer, and he takes off all his clothes in front of other people. Sometimes he'll even dance naked in the street if the money is good."

The teacher is so shaken by his answer that she quickly gives the kids coloring to do and takes David into the hallway to talk to him. "Is that really true about your father?" she asks.

"No," David replies, his face turning red. "He plays for the Toronto Maple Leafs, but I was too embarrassed to say that in front of the other kids."

Q. How do you keep the Washington Capitals out of your yard?

A. Put up a goal net.

A Little Hero

Two young boys are playing hockey on a pond in a park in Toronto, when one is attacked by a rabid Rottweiler. Thinking quickly, the other boy takes his stick, wedges it down the dog's collar and twists, breaking the neck of the vicious dog.

A reporter who happens to be walking by sees the incident and rushes over to interview the boy. "Young Leafs Fan Saves Friend From Vicious Animal," the reporter writes in his notebook.

"But I'm not a Leafs fan," the little hero says to the reporter.

"Sorry. Since we're in Toronto, I just assumed you were," says the reporter, and he starts to write again. This time he writes, "Little Blue Jays Fan Rescues Friend From Horrific Attack!"

"I'm not a Jays fan either," the boy says.

"I assumed everyone in Toronto was either a Leafs or a Jays fan. What team do you cheer for?" the reporter asks.

"I'm a Colorado Avalanche fan," the boy says.

The reporter starts a new sheet in his notebook and writes, "Little Jerk From Denver Kills Beloved Family Pet."

It's All About Perspective

Little Billy arrives home after his hockey game, throws open the door and runs to his dad.

"How was the game, son? How did you do?" asks his father, who was unable to attend the game.

"You aren't going to believe it, Dad!" Billy exclaims. "I was responsible for the winning goal!"

"That's wonderful," his dad says. "How did you do that?"

"I missed my check on the other team's high scorer!"

Q. What do the Dallas Stars and possums have in common?

A. Both play dead at home and are killed on the road.

Where's the Waiter?

A father takes his two hungry sons to a crowded restaurant where hockey fans are watching the Stanley Cup finals on the big screen TV.

The busy waiter takes the father's order, but an hour passes, and the dad and his sons still have no food.

The father is trying to keep his young sons occupied so that they don't get restless, when suddenly they hear shouts of victory erupt from the restaurant.

"Hey!" says the 11-year-old son. "It sounds like someone just got his food."

Growing Up Loving Pink: A Story

Every year, Jim's father asks him what he wants for his birthday, and every year Jim says he wants a pink hockey stick. For years and years this is the only gift Jim ever requests. While other kids want a new cellphone or an iPad, Jim wants only a pink hockey stick. If it is his birthday, he asks for a pink hockey stick, and at Christmas he always asks for a pink hockey stick.

Q: What's the difference between the New York Islanders and a mosquito?

A: A mosquito stops sucking.

Jim's dad tries to tempt his son with the latest "in" thing, but Jim wants only a pink hockey stick.

Eventually Jim's dad gets tired of buying his son pink hockey sticks, so for Jim's 18th birthday, he surprises his son and buys him a brand-new BMW.

Jim likes the car and takes it into town for a spin. As he is driving by a sports store, he sees some pink hockey sticks in the window, so he parks on the side of the road and crosses the street to get a better look. Halfway across the road, Jim is suddenly hit by a truck and is rushed to the hospital. Jim's father goes to the hospital to see his son. The doctors tell Jim's dad that Jim isn't going to make it. The dad wants to ask his son one question before he dies.

"Jim," he says. "You've never played hockey in your life, so why all these years did you want pink hockey sticks as gifts?"

Jim looks up at his father, opens his mouth to speak and then dies.

The moral of the story: you should always look both ways before crossing the street!

Q: Why do Calgary players pour their Gatorade into their jockstraps?

A: It's the only way they will ever drink from the Cup!

A Tough Game

While examining a little boy, a doctor notices that the boy's knees are covered in big purple bruises.

"Do you play hockey or soccer?" asks the doctor.

"Neither," says the boy. "But my sister and I play Uno."

It's Hot in Here!

During an intense practice on the ice, the hockey team's best scorer keeps missing his shots.

The player says out loud, "Wow, it's so hot in here! What couldn't I do with a nice, cold drink!"

The team captain looks at him and says, "Hit it?"

Q: Did you hear? New Jersey is building a new arena but is keeping its location hidden from the public.

A: Yeah, they're afraid the Devils will find out where it is and try to play there.

Don't Be Silly!

In a Boston high school, Darlene is standing in the hallway talking with her boyfriend.

"Sweetheart," she says. "Did you hear the story of the guy who swapped his girlfriend for season tickets to the Bruins games? Would you give me up for anything like that?"

"Now why would I go and do a stupid thing like that?" he replies. "The season is half over!"

Now There's a Thought!

A hockey fan takes his younger sister to a game for the first time, and he answers all her questions about the position of every player.

"Who's that man in front of the net?" she asks.

"He's the goalie," her brother replies.

"And what does he do?" she asks.

"He has to keep the puck from going in the net."

"Oh. And how much is he paid to do that?" she asks.

"About 2000 dollars a week," replies her brother.

"Oh," says the girl. "Wouldn't it be cheaper to board it up?"

Hockey Players in School

Two young hockey players are taking an important final exam. If Alex and Billy fail the test, they won't be allowed to play in the big hockey game the following week. The exam is a fill-in-the-blank quiz.

The last question on the exam reads, "Old MacDonald had a _____."

Alex is stumped. He has no idea what to answer. But he knows he needs to get this answer correct to be sure he passes the test and gets to play hockey.

Making sure the teacher isn't watching him, he taps Billy on the shoulder. "Pssst, Billy. What's the answer to the last question?"

Billy laughs. He looks around to make sure the teacher doesn't notice, then he turns to Alex and whispers, "Alex, you're so stupid. Everyone knows Old MacDonald had a farm."

"Oh yeah," says Alex. "Thanks. I remember now."

Alex picks up his pencil and starts to write the answer in the blank space. Then he stops, taps Billy on his shoulder again and asks, "Billy, how do you spell 'farm'?"

"You are really dumb, Alex. That's so easy. 'Farm' is spelled E-I-E-I-O."

City Kids

Two poor brothers in Chicago are playing with new hockey sticks in the park across the street from their house.

"Hey!" shouts their mother. "Where did you get those hockey sticks?"

"We found them," replies the younger boy.

"Are you sure they were lost?" asks the mother.

"Yes," replies the boy, "we saw some people looking for them just a little while ago."

Chapter 4

Hockey with Adults

Hockey with Adults

Funny parent saying: "If you cook a kid a fish, you'll feed him for a day. But teach a kid to play hockey, and you get rid of him for the whole weekend."

A Silly Dad

A kid hears his dad tell his mom: "I put a sticker of Gary Bettman on my car. Now I keep getting locked out."

Q: Why are goalies good at the Japanese art of origami?

A: Because they're good at working in the crease.

Lockout Tough Times

Subject: An Urgent Plea for Help

With the Christmas season coming up, we ask that you please look into your heart to help those in need. Hundreds of NHL players in our very own country are living at or just below the seven-figure salary level. (Atrocious!) And, as if that isn't bad enough, they won't have a paycheck for several weeks—possibly a whole year—because of the lockout situation. But now, you can get your parents to help!

For only $20,835 a month, which is $694.50 a day (that's less than the price of a large screen projection TV!), you can help a hockey player during his time of need. Your parents' contribution won't solve the problem, as it barely covers the yearly league minimum—but it's a start!

Almost $700 may not seem like a lot of money to your parents, but to a hockey player, it could mean the difference between a vacation spent golfing in Florida or going on a Mediterranean cruise. For your parents, $700 is just one month's rent or one mortgage payment. But to a hockey player, $700 will almost replace his daily salary.

For less than $700 a day, a NHL player can buy a 50-inch TV, trade in his one-year-old Lexus for a new Ferrari or enjoy a weekend in Las Vegas.

The hockey player will be told that he has a *special friend* who wants to help him in his time of need.

Although the player won't know your parents' names, he will be able to make collect phone calls to your home just in case he needs more money for unexpected expenses.

Q: Did you hear about the Polish hockey team?

A: They all drowned in spring training.

So please ask your parents to donate now before another poor hockey player goes without the necessities of life!

Reasons Hockey Is the Best Fighting Sport

- It's like a street gang, but it's organized into teams and the players fight on skates.

- It's okay to punch a guy and slash him with your stick. It's called "part of the game."

- Fans actually pay to see players fight and play a little hockey.

- Hockey violence is better than boxing, and they do it 82 games a year.

- When you get punished for fighting, you get to sit down for five minutes, and then you get to play and fight again.

- Mommies are not allowed on the ice to comfort their battered sons.

- Hockey coaches actually hire players who do not score but instead beat up people.

- Players don't have dental insurance. Actually, a player with a complete set of teeth is unheard of.

- Because of all their stitches, there are no handsome hockey players. They all look like thugs.

Hockey Injury

Wade goes to work one morning, and he is limping something awful. Joe, one of his co-workers, asks Wade what happened.

Wade replies, "Oh, nothing. It's just an old hockey injury that acts up once in a while."

Joe says, "Gee, I never knew you played hockey."

Q: Why was the dumb hockey player so happy after he finished his jigsaw puzzle in only six months?

A: Because on the box it said, "From 2 to 4 years."

"Oh, I don't play," says Wade. "I hurt it last year when I lost $100 on the Stanley Cup playoffs. I got angry and put my foot through the TV."

Overheard at a Hockey Game

Female heckler to the referee: "If you were my husband, you fat, bald bum, I'd give you poison!"

The referee: "Lady, if I was your husband, I'd take it."

Hockey Chatter

Ref: "I'm sending you off!"

Player: "What for?!"

Ref: "The rest of the game!"

Q: What's the best thing about concussions?

A: You keep meeting new friends.

Empty Seat

A young man wins a radio contest and gets the best seat right in front at center line for game seven of the Stanley Cup playoffs. When he gets to his seat, he notices that the seat next to him is empty. A little puzzled by this, he waits until the game starts. When the game begins, sure enough, the seat is still empty. So he asks the old man on the other side of the seat, "Is this seat really empty?"

"Yes," the old man replies.

"Why would someone with a ticket for game seven of the Stanley Cup final not want to come to see the game?" asks the young man.

"Well," the old guy says, "this seat used to belong to my wife. We had season tickets and have never missed a game until she died recently."

Q: Why is it so hot at Carolina Hurricanes games?

A: Because there's not a fan in the place.

"Oh, sorry to hear that. And you couldn't find anyone else?"

"No, I'm afraid not," the old man says.

"So you didn't have any relatives or friends that were available to come to the game? How come?"

The old man looks at him and says, "Because they're all at the funeral."

Hockey Marriage

One man to another, "My wife thinks I put hockey before marriage, even though we just celebrated our third season together."

Superstar!

Old Joe has been retired from the game for many years, but he still likes to tell people how good a hockey player he once was.

"They still remember me, you know," he says to his grandson. "Only yesterday, when I was at the players' entrance, there were a lot of press photographers lining up to take my picture."

"Really?" says his grandson.

"Yes. And if you don't believe me, ask Wayne Gretzky—he was standing right next to me."

Dumb Dumbs

A teenager walks into a restaurant in Toronto, orders a Coke and asks the waiter if he'd like to hear a good Toronto Maple Leafs joke.

"Listen, buddy," growls the waiter. "See those two big guys sitting over there? They were both defensemen for the Toronto Maple Leafs. And see that huge fellow sitting in the corner? Well, he was a fighter for the Leafs in the 1980s. The guy sitting at the counter was the Leafs' all-time champion fighter. And I have also punched a few faces in my years. Now, are you absolutely positive you want to go ahead and tell your joke here?"

Q: Why are the Vancouver Canucks like grizzly bears?

A: Every fall they go into hibernation.

"Nah, guess not," the teenager replies. "I wouldn't want to explain it five times."

Hockey Groom

A young man is getting married and is standing by his bride in the church.

On the floor beside him is his bag of hockey gear.

His bride whispers to him, "What is all your hockey crap doing here?"

The man says, "This isn't going to take all day, is it?"

You Know Your Dad Is an Avid Hockey Fan If...

- His idea of serving breakfast is giving you a fork and dropping an Eggo waffle in the middle of the table.

- He punishes you with "minors," "majors" and "misconducts."

- When he comes to a traffic signal, and the light turns green, he stops.

- When he comes to a traffic signal, and the light turns red, he gets really excited and says, "He shoots! He scores!"

- Instead of duct tape, he uses hockey tape to fix everything.

- He calls a trip to the Hockey Hall of Fame a "pilgrimage."

- He goes into a bank because it advertises "Free Checking." And he walks out disappointed.

- He can pronounce any word in French, but he has no idea what it means.

- Every time he hears a siren he wonders who scored.

- He's not allowed to play chess anymore because the first time he played, he misunderstood the meaning of the word "Check."

- All his clothes are in his team's colors.

- His closet is divided into two sections: "Home" and "Away."

- He always smacks the guy who says, "Check, please."

- He owns a Zamboni. And he keeps it in the garage while his car is parked in the driveway.

- His calendar only runs from October to June.

- He wonders how he will get through July, August and September without hockey.

- When someone says, "Two minutes," he responds, "What for?"

Good Hockey Coach

At one point during a hockey game, the coach pulls one of his seven-year-old players aside and asks, "Do you understand what cooperation is? What a team is?"

The little boy nods his head and says, "Yes."

"Do you understand that what really matters is that whether we win or lose, we stay together as a team?" asks the coach.

The little boy again nods yes.

"So," the coach continues, "I'm sure you know that when a penalty is called, you shouldn't argue, swear or attack the referee. Do you understand all that?"

Again the little boy nods.

The coach says, "And when I take you out of the game so another boy gets a chance to play, it's not good sportsmanship to call your coach 'a worthless idiot,' is it?"

Again the little boy nods.

"Good," says the coach. "Now go over there and explain all that to your parents."

More Money!

A hockey coach at a high school in Detroit storms into the principal's office and demands a raise right then and there.

"Please," says the principal, "you already make more money than the entire math department."

"Yeah, maybe so," says the coach, "but you don't know what I have to put up with."

The coach then takes the principal out into the hallway and says, "Watch this." The coach grabs a sports jock who is jogging down the hallway. He says to the kid, "Run over to my office and see if I'm there." Twenty minutes later, the jock returns, sweaty and out of breath. "You're not there, sir," the kid reports.

"Oh, I see what you mean," says the principal, scratching his head. "I would have phoned."

Q: What has more flames than a BBQ?

A: A Calgary golf course during the playoffs.

Proper English

A friendly hockey game recently took place in Montreal between a group of high school students and a team made up of teachers. Before the game, the two designated captains meet at center ice. They shake hands, and the student captain says, "May the best team win!"

The captain of the teachers, who teaches English, replies, "You mean, may the better team win!"

Dang Parents

A father asks his son what he'd like for Christmas.

"I've got my eye on those special goalie pads in the sports store window," replies the young boy.

"The ones that cost $300?" asks the father.

"That's right."

"Well, you'd better keep your eye on them then— because you're probably not ever gonna play with them," says the dad firmly.

Chapter 5

The Weird Side of Hockey

The Weird Side of Hockey

Definition of the NHL:
A fight where hockey sometimes breaks out.

Who's the Best?

St. Peter and Satan are having an argument one day about hockey and which of them has the best players. Satan suggests that a game be played on neutral ice between a select team chosen by St. Peter and his own handpicked boys.

"Very well," says St. Peter. "But you realize, I hope, that we have all the good players and all the best coaches."

"I know, and that's alright," Satan says. "We have all the referees!"

Q: How can you tell if the ice rink is level?

A: The defenseman is drooling from both sides of his mouth.

Reckless Driver

A Columbus Blue Jackets fan amuses himself by scaring every Pittsburgh Penguins fan he sees strutting down the street wearing an obnoxious hockey jersey. He swerves his car, pretending he's going to hit the guy and then swerves back, just missing him.

Q: Which insect doesn't play well in goal?

A: The fumble bee.

One day while driving along, he sees a priest walking down the street. The driver thinks he will do a good deed, so he pulls over and asks the priest, "Where are you going, Father?"

"I'm going to give Mass at St. Francis Church, about two miles down the road," replies the priest.

"Climb in, Father. I'll give you a lift!" says the driver.

The priest hops into the passenger seat, and they continue down the road. Suddenly, the driver sees a Penguins fan walking down the road, and he instinctively swerves as if to hit him. But as usual, he swerves back onto the road just in time. Even though he is certain that he hasn't hit the guy, he still hears a loud thud. Not knowing where the noise has come from, he glances in his rearview mirror but doesn't see anything. He then remembers the priest is with him, so he turns to the priest and says, "Sorry about that, Father. I almost hit that Penguins fan."

"That's okay," replies the priest. "I got him with the door."

Q: Why did the goalpost get angry?

A: Because the bar was rattled.

A Real optimist

Hockey coach: "Thirty teams in the league...and we finish at the bottom!"

Captain: "Well, it could have been worse."

Coach: "How?"

Captain: "There could have been more teams in the league!"

fun Things to Do with a Zamboni

- Tie rookies to the bumper and drag them around the rink.

- Chase squirrels around the arena parking lot after practice.

- Get a couple of machines and have a drag race.

- Do donuts at the faceoff circles.

- Scare the heck out of the ice-level broadcasters and scorekeepers.

- Take it home and smooth off your backyard ice rink.

- Use it as a moving target for slapshot practice.

- Can you say "Zamboni wheelies"?!

Is that God?

A dumb guy named Earl decides to go ice fishing, so he takes his fishing rod and goes walking around until he finds a big patch of ice. He heads to the center of the ice and begins to saw a hole. All of a sudden, a loud booming voice comes out from above: "You will find no fish under that ice."

Earl looks around, but he sees no one. He starts sawing again. Once more, the voice speaks: "As I said before, there are no fish under the ice."

Earl looks all around, high and low, but can't see a single soul. He picks up the saw and tries one more time to finish cutting a hole in the ice.

Before he can even start cutting, the huge voice interrupts: "I have warned you three times now. There are no fish!"

Earl is now flustered and somewhat scared, so he asks the voice, "How do you know there are no fish? Are you God trying to warn me?"

"No," the voice replies. "I'm the manager of this hockey rink!"

Why You Should Never Attack an NHL Player During a Game

- He's got the stick.

- He's in better shape than you, and he fights for a living.

- He will spit in your eye.

- He has 24 other players from his team out on the ice with him.

- He drinks Gatorade during the game. You drink sugary pop and eat hot dogs.

- The 20,000 other people at the game will find out just how much of an idiot you really are.

Q: Why don't grasshoppers go to many hockey games?

A: They prefer cricket matches.

- You will be featured in television blooper shows and be laughed at for years to come.

- Nobody who looks normal ever does this—have you looked at yourself in the mirror lately?

The Goaltender's Prayer

The puck is my shepherd;

I shall not ice.

It maketh me save in unnatural positions;

It leadeth me into leg splits;

It restoreth my fans' faith;

It leadeth me in the paths of odd-man rushes.

Yea, though I skate in the valley of the

Shadow of the net,

I will fear no sniper,

For my stick is with me;

My facemask and pads they comfort me;

They annointeth my body with muscle cream;

My back-up tippeth over!

Surely coaches and trainers shall follow me

All the games of my life,

And I shall dwell in the house of the Montreal Forum

Forever.

Hockey in Hell

A passionate hockey fan dies and goes to Hell.

A few days later, the Devil goes up to him and says, "What do you feel like doing today? You can have anything you like."

Thinking Hell is not as bad as everyone has made it out to be, the hockey lover says, "Well, I can think of nothing better to do than play a game of hockey. Can we do that?"

"Of course!" says the Devil, and off they go to get changed for the game. Coming out of the dressing room, the hockey player is wearing the best equipment he has ever seen: the sharpest skates, a golden stick and the best pads. The ice is perfect. The hockey player goes out onto the ice and prepares himself for the opening faceoff. He stands there waiting, but nothing happens.

"Come on," he says to the Devil, "drop the puck already!"

"Ah, you see, that's the hell of it," says the Devil with a smile on his face. "We don't have any pucks."

Hearing Angels

The 2004 Stanley Cup playoffs have just ended, and a Calgary Flames fan is walking home from his friend's place, where he has watched

Q: What do you call rodents who play hockey?

A: Rink rats.

his team lose in game seven. He's about to cross the street, when he hears someone whisper, "Don't cross the street. You'll get hit by a car."

When the man looks around to see where the voice came from, he sees a car fly through a red light at just the spot he would have been if he had crossed the road.

"Who are you?" the fan asks.

"I'm your guardian angel," the voice answers. "I prevent bad things from happening to you."

"Wait a second. If you're my guardian angel, you have some explaining to do," the fan replies.

"Ahhh," says the guardian angel. "You want to know why I let Calgary lose. Well, you see—"

Q: When dogs go to a hockey game, what do they like to do?

A: Chase the Zam-bone-y.

The man interrupts the voice and says, "No, actually, I was going to ask where you were when I became a Flames fan."

Spot the Hockey Player

A guy gets robbed on the street and goes to the police to report the crime. He tells the police that he's sure the robber was a hockey player. The police ask him why he would think that. The guy replies, "Because he had no front teeth."

Top Ten Unknown Penalties

10. Kabobbing.

9. Too many men on the linesman.

8. Shucking and jiving.

7. Octopi in the face.

6. Two words: sequined gloves.

5. Illegal use of pants.

4. Doin' the hokey-pokey.

3. Icing the mascot.

2. Two guys, one goalie uniform.

1. Grand Theft Zamboni.

Q: What happens to a hockey player when he becomes blind?

A: He becomes a referee.

NHL Entry Exam

Time limit: three weeks to complete test. You must answer three or more questions correctly in order to qualify for entry into the NHL. Good luck!

1. What language is spoken in France?

2. Write an essay on the ancient Babylonian Empire with particular reference to architecture, literature, law and social conditions—or write down the first name of Barack Obama.

3. Would you ask William Shakespeare to:

(a) build a bridge
(b) sail the ocean
(c) lead an army
(d) write a play

4. What religion is the Pope? (Please choose only one answer.)

(a) Jewish
(b) Catholic
(c) Hindu
(d) Polish
(e) Agnostic

5. How many feet is 0.0 meters?

6. What time is it when the big hand is on the 12 and the little hand is on the 5?

7. How many commandments was Moses given? (approximately)

8. What are people in North America's far north called?

(a) Westerners
(b) Southerners
(c) Northerners
(d) Canadians

9. Spell "Malkin," "Ovechkin" and "Kulemin."

10. Six kings of England were named George, the last one being George the Sixth. Name the previous five.

11. Where does rain come from?

(a) Macy's
(b) a 7-Eleven
(c) Canada
(d) the sky

12. Can you explain Einstein's theory of relativity?

(a) Yes
(b) No

13. What are coat hangers used for?

14. "Oh Canada" is the national anthem for what country?

15. Explain Le Chatelier's principle of dynamic equilibrium—or spell your name in capital letters.

16. Where is the basement in a three-story building located?

17. Which part of the U.S. produces the most oranges?

(a) New York
(b) Florida
(c) Canada
(d) Alaska

18. If you have three apples, how many apples do you have?

19. What does CBC (Canadian Broadcasting Corporation) stand for?

Saying Grace at Dinner

The owners of the Chicago Blackhawks sponsor a banquet for the team's hockey legends. A priest from Chicago is sitting at the head of the table and is asked to say grace before dinner. He must be excited to meet some of the greatest names in hockey because he's a little flustered.

Q: Why did the blonde become a hockey fan?

A: Because every time the clock stopped, she thought she stopped aging.

"Thank you, Lord, for what we are about to eat," he says. He then finishes by saying, "In the name of the Father, the Son and the Goalie Host."

overheard in a Vegetarian Restaurant

"I don't eat anything that has intelligence. On that note, I would gladly eat a hockey player."

Schoolwork

A new hockey player joins a team. A local sportswriter is interviewing the coach and says to him, "The new guy is great on the ice. But how are his school marks?"

"Oh, he makes straight A's," replies the coach.

"Wonderful!" says the sportswriter.

"Yes," agrees the coach, "but his B's are a little crooked."

Q: How do you spot a fake playoff ticket?

A: It contains the word "Columbus."

Pass the Puck

A young guy decides to try out for the local hockey team. "Can you check?" asks the coach.

"Watch this," says the guy, who starts to skate and then smashes into the boards, shattering it to splinters.

"Wow," says the coach. "I'm impressed. Can you go fast?"

"Of course I can skate fast," says the guy. He skates off like a shot, and, in just over 15 seconds, he skates around the entire rink.

"Great!" says the coach. "But can you pass a puck?"

The young guy hesitates for a few seconds and then says, "Well, coach, if I can swallow it, I can probably pass it."

A Brave Man

A man dies and goes to heaven, and St. Peter asks him if he has done any good during his life.

The man says yes. So St. Peter asks the man to tell him about any brave act he has done.

The man says, "Well, I was refereeing a Stanley Cup game in Montreal between Toronto and Montreal. The score was 0–0, and there was only one more minute of play when I awarded a penalty shot for Toronto."

"Yes," says St. Peter. "That was a real act of bravery. Can you tell me when this took place?"

"Certainly," the man replies. "About three minutes ago."

Q: Do you know why the Edmonton Oilers were the last NHL team to get a website?

A: Because they couldn't put three W's in a row.

Mammals Versus Insects

A team of mammals is playing a team of insects. The mammals totally dominate the first and second period and are leading 28–0. However, in the second intermission, the insects make a substitution and bring on a centipede. The centipede scores an incredible 200 goals in the third period, and the insects win the game by a final score of 200 to 28. In the dressing room after the game, the captain of the mammals chats to the insect captain.

"That centipede of yours is terrific," says the captain of the mammals. "Why didn't you play him from the start?"

"We would have liked to," says the insect captain, "but it takes him 45 minutes to get his skates on!"

Toronto Beach

Q: Why are the Vancouver Canucks like Canada Post?

A: They both wear uniforms and don't deliver.

A man is strolling along the beach area in East Toronto when he spots a bottle floating in Lake Ontario. The bottle drifts ashore. He picks up the bottle and opens it, and out pops a genie. "Master, you have released me from my bondage in this bottle. Ask any three wishes, and I will grant them to you."

The man thinks for a moment and says, "I would like the following three things to happen this year: the Toronto Maple Leafs win the Stanley Cup, the Toronto Blue Jays win the World Series and the Toronto Raptors win the NBA title."

The genie thinks about this for a moment and jumps back into the bottle.

A Day at the Hockey Game

Knock Knock!
Who's there?
Hockey!
Hockey who?

Hockey didn't work, so I had to knock!

A doctor at an insane asylum decides to take his patients to a hockey game.

For weeks in advance, he coaches his patients to respond to his commands.

When the day of the game arrives, everything seems to be going well. As the national anthem starts, the doctor yells, "Up, Nuts!" and all the patients stand up.

After the anthem is finished, the doctor yells, "Down, Nuts!" and they all sit back down in their seats.

After the first goal is scored, the doctor yells, "Cheer, Nuts!" and they all start clapping and cheering.

When the referee makes a bad call against the star of the home team, the doctor yells, "Booooo, Nuts!" and they all start booing.

Thinking things are going well, the doctor decides to go get a Coke and a hot dog, leaving his assistant in charge.

When the doctor returns, there is a riot in progress. Finding his assistant, the doctor says to her, "What in the world happened?"

The assistant replies, "Well, everything was going just fine till a vendor passed by and yelled Peanuts!"

Knock Knock!
Who's there?
Puck!
Puck who?

Puck-er up! I'm going to kiss you!

Chapter 6

Your Favorite Teams

Your Favorite Teams

The New York Islanders have a new coach from North Korea: Win Sum Soon.

Bad Smell

A skunk walks into a restaurant, sits down at a table and sees three guys sitting at the next table who are wearing Canucks jerseys. When the waitress walks over to him, the skunk says, "And everyone thinks *I* stink."

Only in Vancouver

The Vancouver police are cracking down on speeders heading into the city. For the first offense, they give you two Vancouver Canucks tickets. If you are stopped a second time, they make you use them.

Dog Fan

At a Toronto Maple Leafs game, a guy says to the man sitting next to him, "Excuse me, sir, I have a question about your dog. I noticed that every time the Leafs score a goal, your dog does a somersault. Why is that?"

The man replies, "I know. It's weird, but I have no explanation."

The first guy then says, "What does he do when the Leafs win?"

"I don't know—I've only had him for 15 years!"

The Habs

A woman is sitting in the arena ready to watch the Bruins and the Habs in Montreal. The players are skating on the ice, getting all primed up for the playoff game.

Q. What do you call a Vancouver Canuck with a Stanley Cup ring?

A. A thief.

A French Habs fan sitting next to the woman asks her in his strong French accent if she knows what the "CH" stands for on the Montreal jersey.

The woman says, "The Canadien Habitants, perhaps?"

The man replies, "No! No! It stands for Center Hice."

Change Needed

When the Toronto Maple Leafs and the Ottawa Senators don't make the playoffs, the management of both teams get together and decide to hold a competition between the two teams because of their great rivalry.

They take all the players to a weekend ice-fishing competition. The team that catches the most fish at the end of the weekend will win a special trophy.

On the first day, after six hours of fishing, the Senators catch 100 fish, and the Leafs have none.

At the end of the second day, the Senators catch 200 fish and the Leafs none.

That night, coach Randy Carlyle of the Leafs gets his team together and says, "I suspect some kind of cheating is taking place."

So the next morning he dresses Phil Kessel in Senator colors and sends him over to their camp to act as a spy. At the end of the day, Kessel comes back to report to his coach.

Q: What is the difference between a Buffalo Sabres fan and a pothole?

A: Most fans would swerve to avoid the pothole.

The coach says to him, "Well, how about it? Are they cheating?"

"They sure are," Kessel reports. "They're cutting holes in the ice."

Typical Flyers Fans

St. Peter is standing at the gates of heaven when a large group of Flyers fans shows up. Never having seen anyone from Philadelphia at heaven's gates, St. Peter says he will have to check with God. After hearing the news, God instructs St. Peter to admit the 10 most virtuous from the group.

Q: Why don't the Anaheim Ducks players drink tea?

A: Because the Montreal Canadiens have all the Cups.

A few minutes later, St. Peter returns to God and says, "They're gone!"

"What?" says a bewildered God. "All of the Flyers fans have gone?"

"Yes," replies St. Peter. "And the Pearly Gates are gone too!"

The Seven Dwarfs

The seven dwarfs are down in a mine when the mine suddenly caves in. Snow White runs to the entrance to the mine and yells out to them.

From deep within the mine, a voice shouts out, "The Jets are good enough to win the Stanley Cup!"

Snow White says, "Well, at least Dopey is alive!"

Q: Why do the Phoenix Coyotes suck at geometry?

A: Because they never have any points.

How the Los Angeles Kings Spent Their Time off after Winning the Stanley Cup

- Joyriding on the Zamboni.

- Skeet shooting on the White House lawn.

- Watching reruns of Ellen.

- You know that adorable skating bunny in the Ice Capades? That was a Kings player!

- Watching the video of the 2012 playoffs 7000 times.

- Making crank calls to Martin Brodeur.

- Playing golf with the Toronto Maple Leafs.

- Drinking milkshakes out of the Stanley Cup.

- Eating!

Newsflash!

Yesterday the Columbus Blue Jackets held their annual "Take Your Daughter to Work Day," and they played a little pick-up game against their daughters. The Blue Jackets lost 15–4.

Help Me!

A teenager is running through the streets of Sunrise, Florida, frantically asking if anyone knows how to cancel a bid on eBay.

A man walking by asks the young man why he wants to cancel his bid.

Q: What is it called when a Florida Panthers player blows in another Panthers player's ear?

A: Data transfer.

The teenager says, "I placed a bid on a Mickey Mouse outfit, and now I'm six minutes away from owning the Florida Panthers!"

An NHL MasterCard Commercial

Season tickets for the Oilers: $1250.

Edmonton Oilers jersey: $120.

Oilers playoff tickets: $500.

Seeing the Oilers eliminate the Calgary Flames: Priceless!

Hockey Season Temperatures: The U.S. and Canada

50°F = 10°C

- New Yorkers try to turn on the heat.

- Canadians plant gardens.

40°F = 4°C

- Californians shiver uncontrollably.

- Canadians try to get a tan.

35°F = 1°C

- Italian cars won't start.

- Canadians drive with the windows down.

32°F = 0°C

- Distilled water freezes.

- Canadian water gets thicker.

0°F = -17°C

- New York City landlords finally turn on the heat.

- Canadians have the last cookout of the season.

-40°F = -40°C

- Hollywood disintegrates.

- Canadians watch movies on DVDs.

-60°F = -51°C

- Mount St. Helen freezes.

- Canadian Girl Guides sell cookies door-to-door.

-100°F = -73°C

- Santa Claus abandons the North Pole.
- Canadians pull down the earflaps on their winter hats.

-173°F = -114°C

- Ethyl alcohol freezes.
- Canadians get frustrated that they can't go ice fishing.

-460°F = -273°C

- Absolute zero; all atomic motion stops.
- Canadians start saying, "Cold, eh?"

-500°F = -295°C

- Hell freezes over.
- The Toronto Maple Leafs win the Stanley Cup.

IQ Test

Albert Einstein arrives at a party and introduces himself to the first person he sees and asks, "What's your IQ?"

The man answers, "241."

"That's wonderful!" says Einstein. "We will talk about the Grand Unification Theory and the mysteries of the universe. We will have much to discuss!"

Einstein then introduces himself to a woman and asks, "What's your IQ?"

The woman answers, "144."

"That's great!" says Einstein. "We can discuss politics and current affairs. We will have much to discuss!"

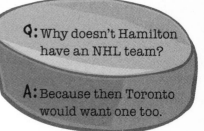

Q: Why doesn't Hamilton have an NHL team?

A: Because then Toronto would want one too.

Einstein goes up to another person and asks, "What is your IQ?"

The man answers, "51."

Einstein responds, "How about them Buffalo Sabres?"

Talking Hockey

Lloyd: "St. Louis should be a better team."

Carl: "Why do you say that?"

Lloyd: "Well, after all, their opponents are always playing the Blues!"

Playing with the Heat

Q: What song do Nashville Predators fans sing before the end of the third period?

A: Nobody knows. There are never any of them left.

One day, Satan is out for a walk through Hell, making sure things are running smoothly. When he gets to the Lake of Fire, he sees a man sitting by the lake, relaxing in a lawn chair. The man is not sweating, and he doesn't look uncomfortable at all. Perplexed, Satan approaches the man and asks, "Young man, are you not hot or bothered by this heat?"

The man replies, "Oh, no, not at all. I lived in downtown Toronto, and this weather is just like a typical July day in the city."

Satan thinks that this is not a good sign, so he rushes back to his office and turns up the heat another 100 degrees. Satisfied with himself, he returns to the Lake of Fire to check on the young man.

When he gets there, the man has a few beads of sweat on his forehead, but that is all. Again Satan asks the man, "Are you hot and uncomfortable yet?"

Q: What does a Calgary Flames player do after he wins the Cup?

A: He turns off the Xbox.

The young man looks up and says, "No. The temperature is just like a hot August day in Toronto. I'm doing just fine."

YOUR FAVORITE TEAMS

Satan decides that he has to do something drastic to make this man's stay very unpleasant. He goes back to his office, turns off the heat and then turns up the air conditioning to max. The temperature quickly drops well below zero. As he approaches the Lake of Fire, Satan notices that it is now frozen over. He also sees the young man jumping up and down wildly, waving his arms and yelling into the air.

"This looks promising!" thinks Satan. Getting closer to the man, he finally hears what he is shouting, "The Leafs have won the Stanley Cup! The Leafs have won the Stanley Cup!"

Q: What do the Calgary Flames and the Calgary Stampeders have in common?

A: Neither can play hockey.

Newsflash!

The New Jersey Devils may have an "evil" mascot, but the Boston Bruins have Satan playing for them!

Seen at a Game

The Washington Capitals coach doesn't stand for any nonsense at his team's games. One Saturday he catches a couple of fans sneaking past security. The coach is furious. He grabs the fans by their coat collars and says to them, "Now you just get back in there and watch the game until it's finished!"

Chapter 7

A Canadian Game

A Canadian Game

Coach to goalie:
You're not Michael Jackson—use your glove!

Half a Loaf

The new stock boy is working in a grocery store in New York City, and a customer approaches him. The customer asks if he can buy just a half loaf of bread. The stock boy says no, but the customer insists he go ask his manager.

The stock boy goes to the manager and says, "Hey, boss, there's some idiot out there who wants to buy half a loaf of bread..." and he turns around to see the customer standing right behind him. Without hesitating, the stock boy says, "and this nice gentleman has offered to buy the other half!"

Q: Did you hear that Ottawa changed its area code?

A: It's now 0-4-3.

The manager gives the customer the half loaf of bread, and the customer leaves the store happy.

Afterwards, the manager says to the stock boy, "That was pretty quick thinking, son. Where are you from?"

The stock boy replies, "Calgary, sir."

The manager says, "Wow, I love Canada! Do you miss it?"

Q: What's the difference between a hockey game and a boxing match?

A: In a hockey game, the fights are real.

The stock boy replies, "Nope! Nothing but hockey players and idiots live in Canada!"

The manager says, "My wife is from Canada."

A CANADIAN GAME

The stock boy replies, "Wow, that's pretty cool! Who did she play for?"

Q: How did the first Frenchman in Toronto get there?

A: He was playing hockey on the frozen St. Lawrence River and got a breakaway.

A Canadian Abroad

A Canadian soldier is walking in a desert when he comes across a magic lamp sitting in the sand. He rubs it and out pops a genie.

The genie promises to give him one wish as a reward for freeing him from the lamp.

The soldier thinks hard and finally takes out a map. He points at a place on the map and says all he wants is to have peace in that war-torn region.

"Wow," the genie says, "that's a tough wish for me to grant. Do you have another wish instead?"

The soldier thinks for a moment and says, "How about the Leafs winning the Stanley Cup?"

The genie replies, "Let me see that map again."

French Canadian Goalie

There is a French Canadian goaltender who loves to wear the number 00 on the back of his jersey. If a curious member of the media ever asks him why he chose those numerals, he always replies, "Every time a puck gets past me, I look back in the net, and I say, 'Oh, oh.'"

Hockey Limerick

With the end of the game in the air,

Every shot on the goal is a scare.

The expletives stream,

As they yell at my team,

"Will you just get the puck out of there!"

A CANADIAN GAME

A Difficult Choice

As in many Canadian homes on New Year's Day, my girlfriend and I face the annual conflict over what is more important: watching Canada's World Junior Hockey team on television or eating dinner with her family. To make my girlfriend happy, I eat dinner with the family, and I even stay at the table for some pleasant after-dinner conversation before rushing downstairs to watch the rest of the game with her brother.

Several minutes later, my girlfriend comes downstairs to give me a drink. She smiles, kisses me on the cheek and asks what the score is.

I tell her it's the end of the second period and that the score is still nothing to nothing.

"See!" she says. "You didn't miss a thing."

Q: What do the Calgary Flames and a girl's bra have in common?

A: They both have two Cups!

Life-long Hockey Buds

Billy and Joe are huge hockey fans.

One day, Billy and Joe make a pact that when one of them dies, the other one will come back in the form of a ghost to let his friend know if hockey is played in heaven.

Sure enough, a few weeks later, Billy dies and appears to Joe as a ghost.

Joe says, "Billy, it's so good to see you! So tell me, is there hockey in heaven?"

"Well," Billy says, "I have some good news for you, and I have some bad news for you. First the good news... yes, there is hockey in heaven!"

"Thank God!" Joe shouts. "What's the bad news?!"

"You're in goal tomorrow."

Apology to Americans from Canadians
(from This Hour Has 22 Minutes)

I'm sorry we beat you in Olympic hockey. In our defense, I guess our excuse would be that our team was much, much, much, much better than yours. As a way of apology, please accept all of our Canadian NHL teams, which one by one are going out of business and moving to your fine country.

Q: Why should you be careful playing against a hockey team of big cats?

A: They might be cheetahs!

Three Things Canadians Can't Live Without

3. Maple syrup.

2. Tim Horton's coffee.

1. Wayne Gretzky.

Hockey Fanatic

"My wife claims I'm a hockey fanatic. She says all I ever read about is hockey. All I ever talk about is hockey. All I ever think about is hockey. I told her she needs to spend time in the box."

Help Wanted

One day when the Los Angeles Kings are playing the Phoenix Coyotes, the referee doesn't show up, so the coach asks if there is anyone among the spectators with referee experience. A man steps forward.

"Have you refereed before?" asks the coach.

Q: Why did the oil company BP hire the Oilers to clean up the oil spill?

A: Because the Oilers will go out there and throw in the towel!

"Certainly," says the man. "And if you don't believe me, ask my three friends here."

"I'm sorry," says the coach. "But I don't think we can use you."

"Why not?"

"You can't be a real referee because no real referee has three friends."

A Hockey Sin

After church one Sunday, a teenager walks up to the priest and says, "Father, is it a sin to play hockey on Sunday?"

"My son," says the priest, putting his hand on the boy's shoulder, "I've seen you play hockey. It's a sin any day."

Q: How many Montreal Canadiens fans does it take to screw in a lightbulb?

A: One to screw in the lightbulb, and three to stand around talking about how good the old lightbulb was.

Chapter 8

Funny Hockey
Quotations & Lists

Funny Hockey Quotations & Lists

Hockey can be funny.
After all, it's the ultimate slapstick sport!

Hockey Players Say the Weirdest Things

- Sometimes the biggest goal of hockey seems to be waiting until the referee's back is turned away so that you can whack your opponent!

- Hockey is like soccer on ice, so maybe it should be called Sock'em!

When he put out his arms to celebrate, the rest of us skated immediately to the bench and left him there all alone.

> –former Los Angeles Kings Dave Taylor on why no teammates celebrated a goal with teammate Marcel Dionne after he received a death threat if he scored twice in a game

I slept like a baby. Every two hours, I woke up and cried.

> –former NHL coach Tom McVie on how he slept after a bad loss

Sometimes people ask, "Are hockey fights real?" I say, "If they weren't, I'd get in more of them."

> –Wayne Gretzky talking about fighting in hockey

My teeth weren't that good to begin with, so hopefully I can get some better ones.

−Blackhawks defenseman Duncan Keith after losing more of his teeth during a game

I will personally challenge anyone who wants to get rid of fighting to a fight.

−Toronto Maple Leafs general manager Brian Burke on the possible elimination of fighting from the NHL

The playoffs separate the men from the boys, and we found out we have a lot of boys in our dressing room.

−former New York Rangers general manager Neil Smith after his team was eliminated from the playoffs

I was a multi-millionaire from playing hockey. Then I got divorced, and now I am a millionaire.

−former Blackhawks sniper and Hockey Hall of Famer, Bobby Hull

I don't want to get into a "he said, she said" with the refs...I'm the he.

−defenseman Chris Pronger

*When I was a kid, I prayed for enough talent to be
a pro hockey player, but I forgot to say NHL, because
they only gave me enough to make the minors.*

–Don Cherry, hockey legend

*Goaltending is a normal job, sure. How would you like
it in your job if every time you made a small mistake,
a red light went on over your desk and 15,000 people
stood up and yelled at you?*

–Jacques Plante, former NHL player

*We get nose jobs all the time in the NHL, and we don't
even have to go to the hospital.*

–Hall of Fame defenseman Brad Park

Every time I get injured, my wife ends up pregnant.

–Chicago Blackhawks Doug Wilson

*Hockey belongs on the Cartoon Network, where
a person can be pancaked by an ACME anvil, then
expanded—accordion-style—back to full stature,
without any lasting side effect.*

–Steve Rushin, sportswriter

Top Ten Reasons Hockey Is the Best Pastime

10. Hockey players wear better uniforms than pro wrestlers.

9. Baseball. Get serious.

8. Real men don't wear figure skates.

7. Golf. Hmm. This one is a toss-up. Both sports involve knocking a hard rubber object into a target with a carbon-graphite stick while wearing hideous clothing.

6. Movie theaters are always as cold as hockey arenas, but they just don't command the same enthusiasm. (And there's no funky chicken in a theater!)

5. Better sound effects than even the coolest video game.

4. Boxing is almost the same sport, but those wimpy boxers do it without skates.

3. Football doesn't have enough violence.

2. Stamp collecting is for referees.

1. When is the last time you went to the ballet and saw a really good fight break out?

Weird Names for Hockey Teams

Chicken Tenders

The Fighting Amish

The Friday Knights

Hat-trick Heroes

Killer Runts

Maple Laughs

Men with Wood

Mighty Molars

Moves Like Jagr

Mud Flaps

No Regretzkies

Names for Women's Hockey Teams

Chicks with Sticks

Goal Diggers

Helmet Honeys

Puck Gals

Skating Babes

The Sweet Spots

Reasons Why Fans Should Not Forgive the NHL and the Players after a Lockout

- Three lockouts in under 20 years!

- Ticket prices keep getting higher!

- Gary Bettman is still the NHL boss.

- The NHL has made billions of dollars, and the fans keep getting asked to buy more stuff and pay more money to see games.

- Cities that don't care about hockey at all have hockey teams (I'm talking to you, New Jersey, Carolina and Florida), and cities that would die to have hockey (Quebec and Hamilton) have nothing.

- Alexander Ovechkin makes more money in one year than your parents do in 10 years, and he still can't score!

- I had to watch basketball to get my sports fix. Basketball, for Pete's sake!

- Guys had nothing to talk about for months.

- Reruns! We had to watch the same TV show over and over again.

- This was my year to win the hockey pool!

Things You Will Never Hear from Fans During an NHL Lockout

- Those poor players. I hope they can pay their bills.

- I think deep down Gary Bettman is a sweetheart.

- You know, I would just love to sit down with Donald Fehr and Gary Bettman and tell them that love conquers all.

- I miss watching the Phoenix Coyotes.

- The players should be making more money.

- This was the Toronto Maple Leafs' year to win the Stanley Cup!

Top Five Excuses of Goalies

5. I slipped on this slippery ice! Someone should put some salt on that!

4. I misunderstood the "butterfly save." I'm sad to report that one less monarch butterfly is flying around.

3. The sun got in my eyes.

2. I misunderstood the use of the trapper. I let in a goal, but now I have a lovely fur coat.

1. Yeah, like you would get in front of that!

Signs of a Bad Draft Choice

10. His guide dog isn't much of a skater.

9. He tells everybody he wants to drink from Stanley's Cup.

8. He's from Cuba.

7. He won't throw a check because he's afraid of breaking his Gatorade bottle.

6. His goalie mask is made from chicken wire, Christmas lights and duct tape.

5. His nickname is "Chicken Cordon Blue."

4. He's throwing up into the goal judge's box—and he has just laced up his skates.

3. When an opponent challenges him to "drop 'em", he pulls down his pants.

2. He uses frozen pucks to chill his cooler of Gatorade.

1. He has all his teeth.

Good Things about Being a Goaltender

- No Halloween costume? No problem!

- Detroit Red Wing goalies look like Santa, so they can make extra money during Christmas.

- You can check out the gals (or guys) on the rink side without them even knowing.

- You can slash all you want—they will send someone else to the box.

- Padding gives the impression you're really buff.

- Your helmet allows you to double as Darth Vader in any new *Star Wars* movie.

- You get cool nicknames, like "Eddie."

- Bruises from flying pucks really bring out the color in your eyes.

Christmas Gift Ideas for Goalies

- SPF 30 sunscreen, for that annoying back-of-the-neck burn.

- A Chia Pet—everyone loves a Chia Pet!

- Ice packs, ice packs and more ice packs.

- Roberto Luongo's newest instructional video: *How to Alienate a Whole City in Three Easy Steps.*

- Tim Thomas' newest instructional video: *Ugly Goaltending Made Easy.*

- Corey Price's newest instructional video: *Riding the Pine with Style.*

- Clothing that brings out the color of his bruises.

Pet Peeves of Hockey Goaltenders

- Fans who throw Hostess Ding Dongs at the net.

- Players who turn their goalie mask upside down and fill it up with chip dip at parties.

- Pads that make their butts look big.

- Jealous back-up goalies that follow them around in the locker room screaming, "Hey, glove *this*, pal!"

- Frostbite caused by a leg split.

- Goal judges at away games who always make wisecracks about burning out the goal lamp.

- Fans who ask, "Can I have your autograph, Mr. Roy?" (Said like it's spelled.)

- Every day, for the rest of their life, they will not have a good reason for dropping anything ever again.

Top Ten Signs that Your Teammate Might be a Rookie

10. He wonders when it's nap time.

9. He thinks being sent down to Moose Jaw is a good thing.

8. He thinks a "road trip" means traveling by bus.

7. Everyone mispronounces his last name, and he doesn't say anything about it.

6. He thinks pre-season games have an "awfully high intensity level."

5. You find him duct-taped to his locker after practice.

4. He thinks the coach is a "pretty good guy"!

3. He actually follows curfew.

2. He freezes up every time he's interviewed and says, "Uhhhh...ummmm...uhhhh."

1. He keeps asking, "Can I drive the Zamboni? Can I? Huh? Can I, please?!"

ABOUT THE AUTHOR

James Allan Einstein has been collecting kids jokes of all kinds since...well...since he was a kid! In fact, he still thinks of himself as a great big kid because he still gets a kick out of grossing people out with vomit and bathroom jokes, and he also loves the quintessential Knock-Knock joke! Invariably, his friends will groan when he says excitedly, "I've got a new one for you!" This book of hockey jokes is especially close to his heart because hockey is his next greatest passion.

ABOUT THE ILLUSTRATORS

Roger Garcia Einstein is a self-taught freelance illustrator who works in acrylics, ink and digital media. His illustrations have been published in humor books, children's books, newspapers and educational material.

When Roger is not at home drawing, he gives cartooning workshops at various elementary schools, camps and local art events. Roger also enjoys participating with colleagues in art shows and painting murals in schools and public places.

Peter Tyler Einstein is a graduate of the Vancouver Film School's Visual Art and Design and Classical animation programs. Though his ultimate passion is in filmmaking, he is also intent on developing his draftsmanship and storytelling, with the aim of using those skills in future filmic misadventures.

Djordje Tordovic Einstein is an artist/illustrator living in
Toronto, Ontario. He first moved to the city to go to York
University to study fine arts. He got a taste for illustrating
while working as the illustrator for his college paper, *Mondo
Magazine*. He has since worked on various projects and
continues to perfect his craft. Aside from his artistic work,
Djordje devotes his time volunteering at the Print and
Drawing Centre at the Art Gallery of Ontario. When he is not
doing that, he is out trotting the globe.

Gerry Dotto Einstein was born and raised in Sherwood
Park, Alberta, where his obsession with the color red led
him to become a graphic designer. Today, he designs using
other colors—not just his favored red.

When he's not at his computer desk, you might find him
playing baseball, watching hockey or dancing down the
street when a good song starts playing on his iPod. Some
people refer to him as the "Mustache Man" for the epic
mustache he sports on his top lip—and when he drinks
chocolate milk, his milk mustache is the king of them all.

Police Justice

A young driver is cruising down the road in Boston and sees two guys wearing Montreal Canadiens jerseys walking on the side of the road. He swerves his truck at the last second and intentionally hits them both. One guy goes flying into someone's front yard, and the other crashes through the windshield of the truck and lands in the passenger seat.

A cop witnesses the accident and pulls over the driver.

"You hit those two guys!" says the cop.

"Yeah, I know," says the driver. "I guess you'll need to make an arrest, right?"

"You bet! I'll charge one for trespassing and one for breaking and entering!"

Mmmmm, Donuts!

A Canadian hockey player named Bobby is walking down the street with a big box of donuts under his arm.

Bobby runs into his friend, Doug, who says to him, "Hey, Bobby! Whacha get the donuts for?"

Q: What do hockey players like most about chess?

A: When they get to check the king.

"I got them for my girlfriend, eh," answers Bobby.

"Oh!" exclaims Doug. "Good trade!"